Prison

Jobs

Now

Providing Care

For

Addicts And Alcoholics?

Mike Wanner

Table of Contents

Introduction

America is a relatively new country compared to the others that have preceded us. We have grown tremendously and have offered a lot to a lot of people but we have had our problems.

We have a number of problems that may get fixed but the quality of the fixes is frequently questioned. We put a lot of people in jail to protect society.

During the creation of this country, there has been a lot of patriotism but also a lot of abuse of our people in both business and the military. The abuses of the past have a kind of societal toxicity which is now surfacing as a dynamic that we do not seem to understand or remedy.

1 - Why I Am Writing This Book

Even in Fantastic Philadelphia there are hard times for many people and optimism may be small. It is time to minimize the hard times and re-inflate the optimistic view by creating a breakthrough in thinking.

A mashup of problems in to opportunity is called for and desperately needed but the possibilities are not understood by many because they have not been conceived until now. I hope that I can share the view that come to me in a way that all can understand.

This book will be unusual as are most of the insights that are coming to me lately. The times are unusual and I hope that now is the time where many things will reset in this country

As always when I write, further insights show up.

The series of rapid thoughts and flashes of possibility that came to me seem like a clear vision that now is the time for change.

2 - Prisons Cost In Many Ways

Prisons are a cost problem for society because there is not a logical plan for ending the costs and the responsibility. The prison environment is generally unsatisfactory for most folks involved with it in any way.

The lives of the incarcerated are not exactly wonderful. There have been many prisoners who complete their service and exit the system but cannot find the kind of forward movement that can offer them lives that support their independence along a positive path of citizenship.

There are many reasons for the way things are and there are logical discussions that clearly declare the reasoning for the absoluteness of the rigidity of the system. Discussions seem to end with finger pointing and universal declaration of how others could or should behave but there seems to be no clear consensus of what should be done.

The motivation for participants in discussions is appropriate for the positions and perspectives of their roles in the big alignment of society as is. Fear plays a part in the perspective also.

There is a need for higher thinking on the part of participants. Ideals are wonderful tools to begin a discussion but management of ideals requires practical determinations.

Some tragic stories are heard about prisoners being released and then committing crimes that hurt people. These reports can stifle the release of other deserving candidates that might be otherwise considered. I hope that all who read this book help to create success stories that carry a positive view.

The major issue that is not discussed very effectively and it is tremendously important is the cost of every aspect of the Jurisprudence system. The bill for all this continues to escalate.

The conversations about costs are complicated and they have a dramatic impact on the efficiency of government because tax dollars spent are gone forever. Government officials have the difficult, if not impossible job, of balancing all the things that determine the quality of life for all the citizens.

The intensity of the emotions behind the issues related to prisons is heavy and consensus is almost impossible to achieve.

3 - Addiction Realities

Those who are addicted to substance are in a constricted negative spiral, like prisoners, because they are also not looking forward to a bright future. I am talking about both Addicts and Alcoholics and the programs that flow from these ideas could be separate programs or a joint program depending upon many variables.

The insight of this writing has me aware of the differences of resources within the care giving communities, the damage to communities' sense of safety by those that are seeking what they feel they need, and the pattern of negativity that spirals down the hopes and ambitions of all who witness the travesty.

Pharmaceutical Drugs have been created to help the healing of so many struck with illness and disease. This beneficial development has been marginalized by the illegal use of these formulations for sensational non-medical highs.

Furthermore, profit seekers have further corrupted the situation by creating unregulated substitutions that are not controlled professionally in the manufacturing process and labeled according to medical standards

Illegal Drug manufacturers have even been known to package products in a way that makes them more appealing to children so that unsuspecting new customers can get hooked without even knowing that they took a risk.

The unlabeled drugs are even a bigger problem because any one who takes them and subsequently seeks medical attention will be entrapped in an information void that could easily take their life.

Legal formulations are precisely marked so that health care practitioners can react to medicine reactions in a precise appropriate manner that can save the life of a patient. When dosage values are distorted or non-existent, there is a risk created that can make it almost impossible for care practitioners to remedy reactions and save lives.

Whether drug addiction started through legal drugs or illegal drugs, the high of substance creates the appearance of an ever increasing "need" to have more and starts an unsustainable cycle which leads to the shortening of lives. Chronic inappropriate Drug use can shorten lives.

Efforts to help people with addiction is stifled by an absence of support resources. Also, the more time that drugs have been used may decrease the likelihood of success.

There is a clear difference between traditional medical diagnosis and conditions related to substance.

The pattern of medical care is well established and the need for cost containment becomes even more apparent in the current economic times so rapid change seems unlikely. We could perhaps get creative and that is why I am writing.

A lot of people need help and there is help available but the lives of those with challenges are very fragile and timing is critical. The ideas that I am suggesting here will not replace any existing programs but they could offer hope that matters to a great number of people and especially those that have been recently detoxed and released from medical facilities who might likely regress if returning to the neighborhood where their addiction started or grew.

My hope here is that three communities can get significant support with a very basic effort to provide a creative alignment in a unique way. Jobs and careers for prisoners in a fee for service budget environment that adds time to withdraw from substance for medically cleared candidates who need nothing more than the support of friendly facilitators.

By the way, the hope is that the program can also provide skills for prisoners who will be released so they can find employment with their new skills once they have served their time.

4 - Fear Realities

Life can be cruel and a lot of defensiveness is really about fear and the answer to fear is rooted in an opposite vibration called love. As you read that, the degree to which the threat of addicted persons stresses you is likely a good indicator of the power of fear that is within you.

I invite readers to go within and check it out. I have a whole website for stress that is free and I invite you to visit http://www.StressReleaseCoach.com and just dip in to some ideas that may bring you some peace. The site is not about addiction, just stress.

Prisoners can have fear but they also seem to have a disconnect because their imprisonment was not in their plan and they are trying to cope but it is not really simple to do.

Of course, fear is a consideration for the whole rest of the community and that is the justification offered for the isolation that is in between the people and the prisoners.

Now there is a new fear which may help to provide a base upon which change can be built. The new fear is economic and the whole country and the world are involved.

Economic chaos is forecast by governmental units and anybody who studies economics can tell you there is reason for concern and something has to change but nothing seems to happen. Financial pressure could be relieved somewhat if Prison costs could be better controlled.

In America alone there are more that 2.3 million people in jail including roughly some 1,351,000 state prisoners in some 1,710+ state prisons, 211,000+ federal prisoners in 100+ federal prisons and 34,000 youth prisoners in 940+ juvenile correctional facilities and some 646,000 local prisoners in some 3,280+ local and tribal jails.

According to a stunning report issued by CasaColumbia at Columbia University, " 65% of All U.S. Inmates Meet Medical Criteria for Substance Abuse Addiction, Only 11% Receive Any Treatment" NEW YORK, N.Y., February 26, 2010

I highly recommend reading the gift that Columbia has shared. The statistics are scary and they further report that "…alcohol and other drugs are significant factors in all crime."

The authorities are producing the figures and our society is hiding from the fact that addiction is out of control. We as a society need to be realistic and take charge and it will take all of us to do it.

Change is needed and the time is now. The thing that makes the most sense is to move prisoners from a liability to productivity. I have shared some figures but I am not an accountant and have no idea about how to factor all of this.

The damage to communities' sense of safety by resistance to those that are seeking what they feel they need is very clear and sad. Also sad is the pattern of negativity that spirals down the hopes and ambitions of all who witness the travesty of addicts, alcoholics and prisoners.

5 - From Blame to Revision

When problems exist, many people want to blame industries, companies and individuals for the problem. Assigning blame has no value in a cultural situation. It is not like an auto accident.

It is like we all live in a boat called our society and we sink or swim together. We need to plan, design and implement remedial actions that can make possibilities better in the immediate, short run, annual and long term future.

The only way forward is not a Band-Aid but a revision.

The basic proposal for consideration here is in a rudimentary format as the expertise needed for success is not in me. The expertise needs a foundation which must be created in order that change be facilitated.

The foundation can only be created with an attitude shift at many levels to make the impossible possibile. If you have read this far then you perhaps are a key person in creating new possibilities.

6 - The Prison Crisis

Unless there is breaking news that I missed, the spiral of human misery in our prisons continues to deteriorate the lives of all those who are in any way effected by the system. Some hopeful stories hit the press and show glimpses of possibilities but in general, it seems that bleakness prevails.

Improvement cannot grow from infrequent episodes of human kindness in a field of utter despair. What is needed is a deliberate re-initiation of the institutions that governments control and a pattern of logic that can justify initiatives to the public.

While this can be summed up in a few paragraphs, the skills of large teams will be needed to dot the I's and cross the T's to create a plan that will make things different. Alas and unfortunately system change is not likely until some thinking changes are integrated.

7 - The Substance Abuse Issue

It is not hard to find headlines about the addictions crisis so I will not bore you with details that you can readily find out about in your hometown. I will recap some problems that I see with people who need care and I am not writing as an expert but merely as an observer of issues that seem to be a detriment to many communities.

It seems that significant issues are:

1. Addiction is not seen as a normal part of health care and there are not sufficient resources available for treatment.

2. There is a great focus on personal freedom and resistance to taking action against candidates for care.

3. Addiction is multi-leveled and not easily proved during the stages when it is most effective to take remedial actions.

4. There is a cultural dynamic that portrays many with issues as cool and even enviable.

5. There is a Macho Perspective which is not helpful.

6. By the time that people are asking for help, efforts can already be too late to create effective change for some.

7. The damage done by street drugs can be much more detrimental and costly to society than giving away huge volumes of other services to the population in order to stem the tide of community deterioration. Can we please take a long view of community building.

8. Many stories are about our Veterans being involved with street drugs because the relief they seek is not working to the level of relief that they feel they need.

9. TV producers are excellent at selling violence and sex in a graphic visual media using yesteryear standards. I hope that every great director can find some time to mastermind with universities about value education joint efforts to create dynamic vibrant possibilities for the minds of those who otherwise might be bored and destroyed by toxic thinking.

8 - Safety and Security

This draft is in no way compliant with the safety and security that citizens would expect a government to initiate. Alas and unfortunately, the real life situation for governments is equally unattractive.

Governmental agencies have many resource challenges and the ones most seriously impacted are limited resources for the children and the needy. It is the hope and intent in this writing that new opportunity can be found to decrease the demands on government so that the programs that choose are able to be adequately funded so the children and the needy are served well.

Cautions are Many

1. The author has resisted many thoughts but the content that keeps coming is begging for fresh ideas to be shared.

2. Please know that I understand fully that many people do not share the understanding that improvement is possible. Already, I have heard the naysayers and I respect both the political and other beliefs of all.

3. I have no agenda except to share what I believe that has been given to me to share. I claim no authority and no offer except an idea to be evaluated by all those that have superior knowledge and wisdom in the areas discussed.

4. I do understand that the priorities of governing are difficult and would personally not want to make the decisions that I am suggesting for consideration. Times continue to be tough and may get tougher yet.

5. I do not claim any sanctity or philosopher like status. I am a human like you trying to do the best I can.

6. Please know this is not a government give out program. This is a modification plan that might help some specific people if it is reviewed and initiated in a format customized for any given areas or institutions as meets the needs there. This is a beginning concept.

7. I suggest that oversight be initiated to insure the integrity of the effort. Forensic accounting and professional supervision are recommended.

8. The stakeholders in any programs will likely have higher success rates if Union representatives, business leaders, and family members participate.

9. There may be value if review boards be established to cross evaluate efforts.

9 - The Goals

The goals of the program are to:

1. Establish changes to the prison situation for the benefit of prisoners, guards, prisoner's families, guard's Families, addict's families and all involved with prisons and addictions.

2. Establish new resources for those with addiction issues that are basic at the beginning.

3. Establish the benefits above through multiple efforts by families, businesses, non-profit groups and others interested in the benefits laid out in #1.

4. Provide a constant revenue neutral situation where cost savings and cost acceleration avoidance are provided for the institutions, governments and taxpayers of involved governments.

5. Supervision as needed.

10 - The Basic Plan

The Startup Plan would be:

1. Adoption of a working plan that would allow for a non-profit organization to be created for the education, rehabilitation and employment of prisoners in a system to be created for the treatment of addicted and/or alcoholic individuals in a contained environment.

2. The benefits to the prisoners to be negotiated with the authorities before any services would commence.

3. The benefits to the addicted/alcoholic person who would receive the care to also be negotiated with all participants before any services would commence.

11 - Considerations for Prisoners

The success of this plan will take initiative from prisoners like you but also acceptance of the initiatives submitted.

You and this plan could prove that options are appreciated, possible and collectively beneficial.

Your imprisonment may be something that you regret from a personal standpoint but also something that a part of you may see as unjustified. Whatever you have thought for years is now worthy of release. You have the possibility of a fresh start on a new life track and yesterday's baggage towards yourself or others will not help you be successful on this critical leg of your new journey.

If you desire better tomorrows for yourself and others, it is important that you do the work to make that possible right away. Each of us has a limited amount of days and your success will be earned so that you can be proud of it. Fear not, just work towards the opportunity if it is offered.

It might be helpful for you to prepare yourself for the people that you will help. This will not be easy but the rewards can bloom new life in to your days. When I want something to work out, I like to pray. You might like that also.

I wish you success in your life and this program and it is my hope that your future will bring you many new freedoms. I also hope that your performance will change the lives of many who will also have a chance for a new start because you have done a great job.

12 - Considerations for Addicts/Alcoholics

Addicts and their representatives will need an awareness that the program is dependent on the interests of many people being served. Every citizen and taxpayer has an interest in things working out.

Please understand that participation will require you to surrender your freedom and that can be very key for you to reach a level of clear thinking that can help you change your life. If you are considering this level of care, you might need the isolation in order to reach your optimal personal power.

Even if you have been spoiled and protected your whole life, this program will not do that for you. If you drop out here - there will likely be little hope left for you in the real world that has value and satisfaction.

If you are going to apply to participate, please know that like never before – you are running out of opportunities and this may be your last.

13 - Considerations for Prison Authorities

Criteria for Facilitators to consider:

1. No Favoritism

2. Real Community Value

3. Progress on a limited basis so that there are no disruptions to the careers of talented professional correction officers.

4. This idea will be highly controversial so early consensus building is important to provide peace.

5. Safety for your correctional officers can be increased.

6. Hope and joy can bring great peace to your facility.

7. Efficiency and peace are indicators of good management.

14 - Criteria for Organizers

We will need to have motivated individuals who have:

1. A vested interest in the success of the program.

2. A separation from those involved in the program that they are monitoring.

3. The ability to communicate effectively through policy rules.

4. Success of the initiative can lead to further systemic growth.

5. Your interest in the welfare of prisoners or addicts or alcoholics can lead to much more goodness in society that can benefit many people.

15 - Summary & Plan for Project

The first part of this proposal would be to create economically viable options that would fulfill these target goals:

1. Create Viable options for minorly addicted folks to find an affordable program that could help them have the constricted environment needed to keep them from easily falling in to surrender to their cravings while they are not thinking clearly.

2. Create options for Use of their Moral Integrity for prisoners who want to change their lives but have virtually no options to do so.

3. Reduce the population, intensity and risks of prison environments where there are no opportunities to create healthier opportunities for their lives by doing hard work that could lead to recognition, appreciation and future success as a contributor to society.

4. Stabilize taxes and risks and benefits through Creative Application within constitutionally declared responsibilities.

5. Save lives of Guards, Prisoners and patients suffering with addiction patterns and the problems caused thereby.

The Starting point needs to have built in compatibility for all participants and a plan of monitoring and supervision which must include:

1. Planning Committee

Planning meetings prior to initiation to determine the priorities of all participants.

2. Determination of Ideal Participants at all levels:

A sponsor to fund the initial expenses of one participating prison organization. Sponsor could be involved with the organization but the initial ideal candidate would be an agent for a Benevolent Organization that is disconnected from participating agencies.

An agency to provide the prisoner participants.

An agency to provide the contacts with those who have addiction.

An agency with the skills and resources to provide professional supervision

3. Site Selection Committee

4. The devil is in the details so all participants need to dialogue and determine what is next and a timetable to match each item.

16 - End Of Concept & Some History

Money Still Talks

Once upon a time in America, there was a thing called prohibition and that prevented people from getting alcoholic spirits in a legal way. That situation created great risks to society and especially law enforcement.

People who were determined to get these beverages took all kinds of risks to satisfy the craving that motivated them. They did things that they should not have done and hurt people who got in their way. The situation was not good.

Eventually it seems there was a determination that the masses of people would break the laws and that the cost of enforcement was too high to justify. A moderated position where the wanted product was available legally has allowed a legal window where adults could purchase what they wanted without risk of police action.

While I am not making a recommendation that the restrictions on drugs be legalized to the same extent as alcohol, I am suggesting that law enforcement needs protection from risks that make the cost of enforcement too high. The war against drugs seems somewhat counter-productive if not futile as the pushing against seems to be increasing the appetite for drugs much like prohibition did for alcohol. Like alcohol illegality is not a barrier to availability but it does fill prisons.

A further complicating factor in the issue of illegal drugs is the impact of entertainment media and video games that seem to have a kind of counter-culture sophistication that leaves the youth of today seeing purveyors of violence and drugs as a kind of hero in business that is difficult to rationalize but the existence of it is a factor.

I would urge the authorities to look seriously at options that would curb risks to society and police.

All things are relative and addicts and prisoners could use options that are yet to be manifested.

Another factor in the illegal drug scenario and addiction in general is the use of substance by veterans in their great struggle called life.

17 - Wrap Up

Every Human struggles and gets lost in the frenzy of life so it is not at all unusual that society can develop also in an off target approach that seems to follow directly. Periodically evaluations can indicate that the target is being missed and reassessment is necessary. This is one such time.

The ideas expressed here are dramatically contrary to the normal security seeking patterns regulated by fear. There is a lot at stake here and the traditional patterns while logical are also unproductive and bankrupting us.

We are at a crossroads in the lives of the addicts and the alcoholics and the prisoners and we are also at a crossroads in the lives of the poor and starving children and also middle income families. Change is not only necessary but required. Absent Change, more misery is our destiny.

I do not know that the changes suggested here are an answer or just a first step or a trial balloon. I have tried to share what has come to me and now I transfer responsibility to those reading as you also are in this problem and the possibilities.

Do you want to change? The question is futile because we all know the answer is – NO.

The obvious next questions is will you change? The Answer is not so certain!

I sincerely hope that you see the sincerity of this document and I hope this writing hits the mark needed to improve lives.

We will have many days ahead and you get to determine how well they will be. Your power is more significant than you probably realize.

Even if your thoughts this minute are full of fear, you have power. A power frequently underappreciated is prayer because even if it changes nothing else, it changes you.

I have to think back to history again and reflect on some significant events. In 1492, Columbus set out on an adventure that forecast his vessel falling off the end of the earth. The end of the story worked out differently and well for many.

Once upon a time. England had a great problem with prisoners like we do now. England banished them to a foreign land where these unwanted people created a great land of their own and now the Queen visits them.

We can have fifty versions of new constricted environments that will maximize freedom, control risks, optimize and reorganize lives. Let freedom ring again with enough control.

The war is only lost if we surrender by giving up our power to fear. I encourage all readers to open their minds to the field of potential that flows from avoiding fear and following reasonable options that help everybody else do the same.

Blessed Be all of us and the new future that we can create together.

*

Inspiring Quote

"We are each of us angels with only one wing, and we can fly only by embracing each other."

~Lucian De Crescenzo

Mike Wanner

Mike worked for Sears Roebuck and Co. while in High School and after graduation until he joined the U. S. Air Force in 1965. He went through Technical School in Wichita Falls, Texas for Aircraft Maintenance One & Two Engine Jets and spent a year on the flight line working on T-38's.

They sent him off to technical school again at Chanute Air Base in Rantoul, Illinois where he studied Maintenance Control Systems. He was assigned to the Precision Measurement Equipment Laboratory in Lubbock, Texas and was the NCOIC of Laboratory Scheduling for Electronic, Electro-Mechanical, Hydraulic and Radioactive Test Equipment.

He went to Vietnam after that and was the Precision Measurement Equipment Monitor for Nhatrang Air Base.

He returned to Sears from Vietnam in 1969 and stayed until 1978. His final Sears assignment was as an efficiency expert in Methods - Operational Research and Development.

He started a private ambulance company in 1975 and worked professionally in the field until 2001 when he devoted his full attention to real estate investing, healing, coaching and eventually writing.

In 2012, Mike became a Certified Professional Coach by The Master Coaching Academy and Joined The Personal Empowerment Group.

He volunteers for local non-profit agencies in the Philadelphia area. His websites are StressReleaseCoach.com and ReverendMikeWanner.com.

www.ingramcontent.com/pod-product-compliance
Lightning Source LLC
Chambersburg PA
CBHW070245290526
45789CB00004B/1769